THE ONLY TRUTH

OH REJOICE, FOR THIS IS THE RE-BEGINNING OF THE NEVER-ENDING

EASHWARRAN KOHILATHAS

CONTENTS

BHAGAVAN

The Age of Non-Duality is Upon Us.
Om Namah Shivaya
Om Namah Para Brahman
Amen
I am "I".
I am I am.
I. am.
Ohm.
Aum.
ॐ
ओम्
ௐ
1
0
...

I'M NOT HERE TO CONVINCE YOU

If the breath in your lungs cannot convince you,

Who am I?

EVOLVE OR GO EXTINCT

It is likely that there has never been any other time on this planet where so many are realising that mankind is in a little bit of a pickle.

Whether it's a financial recession, wars, environmental pollution, corrupt politics, global authoritarianism, a health crisis, or food shortages, it feels like there is something to be worried about. More concerningly, these problems seem bigger than us and aren't going away.

And you will be right to be worried. However hard one may try to ignore these problems, however hedonistically and in deep denial one chooses to live in the face of danger, these problems won't magically disappear overnight. If we don't face them, then our children and their lineage will have to. That is, if they'll be alive and able to do so by then.

Remember that these are humanitarian problems; yes, the environment will suffer for a little while, but the Earth will continue to spin whether or not humans are on it. So a case can be put forward arguing that it's in humanity's best interest to look for solutions.

Many have noticed this looming darkness, and in efforts to

combat these growing catastrophes, we have done what we have always done and have always been good at: research the problem, form groups, endlessly complain about the issue, demonstrate, or spend years trying to bring perpetrators to justice.

Yes, some material progress has been made by doing what humans have always done, but in the grand scheme of things, it's done nothing. In fact, more people are unhealthy and unhappy now than ever before.

The principal problem is that we've been trying to fix and staple back the diseased leaves of a dying tree. Scrambling over ourselves, hoping that by fixing one branch or one leaf, the whole tree will heal. But that's not how life works. To find real solutions, one must fix the root cause. The root.

Once this is fixed, all other problems vanish, and one may enjoy the shade provided by the healthy tree.

Charities, environmental groups, and other similar organisations, even those with the best interests at heart, are useless if the root cause isn't addressed. In fact, these groups perpetuate the problem.

The only way mankind may find any real solutions to the problems it faces today is when it understands that what it has been doing all this time has been useless and has in fact caused the problem in the first place.

The only way we can even begin to ensure our species is safe is through individual psychological revolutions. A total transformation of how we approach life and problems. A total transformation of ourselves.

At the end of the day, there are only two choices.

We either evolve or go extinct.

NO ONE IS GOING TO SAVE MANKIND

No one, no group, no religion, no God, no pill, no technique, no law, no rule, no politician, no political party, no organisation, and no movement will ever save mankind.

To think that the answer lies externally is a trick of the mind, a trick conditioned in us for thousands of years, primarily over the last 100.

The externalisation of responsibility works hand-in-hand with authority-seeking behaviour, both of which are again due to thought, by its very nature.

One must approach thought itself differently, with unwavering, non-judgmental curiosity, to fully appreciate the creature that it is.

Thought is not mere instructional words that pop up in our brain correctly at the right time, but a complex narration of ideas and a reflection of an internal state of affairs moulded through cultural, physiological, and psychological conditioning. It is reliant on, and forms, memory and knowledge, both of which are finite and thus incomplete.

Thought, an evolutionary vital tool that has allowed humankind to survive life on Earth, has however been overused in recent times and used at the wrong times. Moreso, thought has no idea how to deal with issues of the internal.

It only knows what it knows, so to find solutions to real psychological and social problems, it does what it has always done, look externally.

But thought will never be able to solve the hard questions of life, and thus no group or anything external will be able to find solutions to human suffering.

Thought is stuck, though. “If not I, then what else can solve these problems?” It thinks to itself, unaware that the problems created are rooted in *it,* and is unwilling to *not* be part of the solution.

If humankind does not understand that all the real problems of life are rooted in thought, then we may get to Mars in fancy spacesuits (that is, if humankind doesn't kill ourselves in the process), but it’ll be having the same wars, internal conflict, and suffering that plague us today.

All external so-called “progress” is useless if no change has occurred within.

No one and no external thing is going to save us.

Only you can save yourself.

HUMANS ARE IRRATIONAL CREATURES

When the Ego is not examined, man is bound by ignorance, not knowing his True Self. This ties him to duality, endless suffering, and confusion.

The Ego, using thought, which by its nature is incomplete, finite, and subject to conditioning, only further binds man to suffering.

The more trapped the individual is, the further they veer away from their True Self. This increased thought-centred suffering is the cause of all internal conflict and mental illness.

All blind to their True Nature are objectively irrational, hypocritical, and confused.

Saying one thing and doing another is the definition of irrationality.

You are either lying to yourself or not. There is no middle ground.

When the intensity of irrationality increases, darkness ensues, but never complete darkness.

Trauma, ignorance, and a lack of love all feed into this darkness.

Here, the false self, the Ego, begins to attack its own perception of self. One may lose control over one's reality. One may begin to fragment one's personality and idea of gender. Fear takes control.

See, flailing around trying to look for answers, thought, not knowing that it is the root of the problem, can only do what it knows best: fragment and divide.

As we are the world and the world is us, this inner confused consciousness is reflected outwardly.

Modern society.

THE WORD IS NOT THE THING

How does one describe the colour red to someone who is blind? In that way, words become meaningless in describing the Truth I'd like to try and share with you.

The understanding and, thus, change needed to occur in individuals for humanity as a whole to subvert extinction are impossible to put into words. This or any other book will never be enough.

If it were as easy as writing down what needed to be done and following it, then we wouldn't be here in the first place.

Primarily, words, though useful, are never able to grasp the true essence of a thing. The word "tree" is not a tree, and so on. The word is not the thing.

In fact, words, if written, are symbols made up of shadows and differences in colours that evoke memories and thoughts within the brain. It is thought—the very thing one must understand. Words, by evoking thoughts, may then trap the individual in a cycle of non-understanding.

For total understanding, one must understand understanding itself. This, though seemingly elusive to arrive at, is possible. In fact, the simplicity and obviousness of it are what make the whole ordeal difficult and impossible for most. And in the same regard, quite funny once seen.

One may grasp a concept on an intellectual level but not truly understand it. Take Infinity; the mind cannot grasp the concept of infinity. If an infinite number of books were to be written in an infinite number of languages and placed in an infinite number of libraries, they would still not be able to reach the essence of Infinity. This is the shortcoming of the mind.

What I am trying to communicate transcends words. What I am trying to communicate exists in another realm, a realm that requires action. To learn how to ride a bike, one must go out and get on a bicycle. Reading about it is not enough.

So see words for what they are, useful signposts, but do not get caught up in the web of thoughts. Change requires action. Real change requires careful attention. Take nothing written here as advice or gospel. Understand understanding.

FREEDOM IS ATTAINED THROUGH UNDERSTANDING

From the cosmic to quantum scales of existence, nothing has free will. Not you, not me, not the elephant, or the flower. We do not have control over the heat of the sun, when the rain falls, who our parents are, what neurochemicals our brains create, or the breath that keeps us alive.

However, an illusion of free will exists that allows us to live in this realm. Between two types of food, we pick one, and though we had no choice in the matter to begin with, the fact that we *think* we do keeps society running as it is.

One can take the lack of free will, in all senses, as an unchanging variable. And thus, in day-to-day life, this variable is ignored.

The fish, seemingly, do not know that they are swimming in water, which is keeping them alive. We can assume they live, not knowing water exists. But water exists.

If an individual believes he has total free will over his actions, he will get into a rut and live a life of contradiction. His life is a result of his actions, or so he thinks, and thus he will take it upon himself to chase "better" decisions and live internally hypocritically when his will and outcomes do not match. He will suffer.

The fish do not know they live in water, but what if they did? The same question applies more pertinently to man, as man has higher capabilities for understanding greater complexities.

As far as we know, man is the only species on the planet that is capable of grasping this Only Truth. This is because man specialises in understanding and is capable of higher thinking. But to be fair, how could and why would we know or need to know any differently? Your consciousness is only yours. Your journey is an individual one.

One can say that "awakening" is the realisation that one ultimately has no free will. We are like twigs in a flowing river. We move, and most of us live and die thinking that we are moving ourselves, but in reality, it is life, or the river, that moves us.

In Ultimate reality, whether or not someone awakens is not down to their control but already written in cosmic law. But as stated earlier, we may ignore this unchanging variable for now, as we have no illusory control over it.

So why does man, with his capabilities, struggle to grasp this Only Truth? Well, the problem is that man confuses the tools used to navigate the external world with those used to explore the inner world. The problem is that man thinks.

Freedom is attained through understanding, but this understanding is not achieved through thinking.

THOUGHT

Thought exists as a system, not as an independent entity. When most of us think about thinking, we generally only refer to its content but fail to understand that it is more than this. The context, structure, and rate of thought are other equally important features of thought and are vital determinants of not only its quality but that of the organism and the surrounding environment as well.

Thought is not separate from the organism. There is a bidirectional relationship between it and the creature thinking and, thus, an undivided holistic relationship between it and everything else.

One must also note that, though seemingly occurring out of randomness, this is not how thought works. Thoughts arise somewhat as a reflex to sensations while also causing sensations. And thus, one may see thought as the cortical interpretation of the internal and external environment.

We know, but frequently forget, that thought has an emotional quality. Some thoughts are happy, and others are sad, etc. Thought signals emotional centres, which in turn feed back to areas of thinking - a loop is formed - and this may in turn lead to learned behaviours revolving around emotions, chronic pain, etc.

As well as this, thought, by its very nature, fragments, compares, and holds memory. This constructs psychological time.

Like the nose in front of our eyes, we have learned to ignore thought. We are all so used to thinking that we don't even know we are thinking when we are.

Most importantly, we fail to realise that who we think we are is also a construction of thought.

We have turned thought's comparative and fragmentary properties inward and falsely separated ourselves from everything else. It forms the "self."

When do you feel most "at one" with everything? When thought disappears.

The "self" is a natural state of affairs, probably arising to protect the body, which houses the mind, aiding it to navigate the world. Due to its fragmentary nature, one may say that all thought is a form of fear. I am using fear here to describe subtle subconscious unrest, all the way up to the more conventional meaning of the word.

Fear is needed for survival and determines wants, needs, and when to fight or flee. And through this supposed division of the internal and external, the "self" is constructed.

So it may be fair to assume that to find the true nature of consciousness, the thing that exists behind thought, one must remove all fear, inflammation, and blockage.

Remember, thoughts are a reflection of the internal state of affairs; greater disruptions lead to greater turmoil, the fragmentation of one from others, and even the fragmentation of the "self" itself.

This may be at the root of all known mental health issues.

The bombardment of sensations, whether arising internally, externally, or within the system, is noise and creates noise. Quietness is the mind in homeostasis, or "order". A state where fear disappears.

So to find one's True nature, interconnectedness is needed. The symbiosis of various regions of the brain, the body, and our interaction with the external world likely form stronger overall communities. This wholeness reflects quietness. This is done by truly understanding thought.

To make matters more interesting, one must reflect on the fact that, though sensations and thoughts seem to arise from a vector point of this seeming "self," on closer analysis one learns that there is no "one" experiencing all of this.

We are so accustomed to thinking that it isn't questioned or explored in modern society. In fact, thinking is heralded as important and obvious. "I think, therefore I am."

So who, or what, are you when no thought is present?

THERE IS ONLY LOVE OR FEAR

There is only love or fear. And there must be that way.

Before I continue, I must note what I mean by the terms "love" and "fear". When I describe fear, I mean anything that causes internal unrest, whether excessive or not, whether appreciated or not. Fear is that many headed serpent branching from one undiscovered area of misunderstanding. Fear is envy, fear is anxiety, fear is competition, and fear is authority seeking. Fear is not calling your mother when you know you need to. Fear is not speaking up at a meeting at work when you know some wrongdoing is going on. Fear is calling yourself fat. Fear does nothing about it.

When I describe love, I am talking about living in the now, the only thing that exists. I am talking about an emotion that is not led by words, but by feeling. It's staying behind with a friend to help them out even though you know you'll be late. It's getting lost in smelling a rose or listening to music. It's the emotion that is evoked when one understands that one is part of the Infinite. It's listening. It's forgiveness.

Both of those exist on different sides of polarity. Both of them form reality. It is just made that way, just like a magnet has a positive and negative pole. They are dual in nature, just like the sun and moon, like daytime and nighttime. If there was no daytime, there would be no night, and then, by definition, there would be no daytime. The past must exist for the future to exist. A wave must go up and down. Reality ceases to exist if this movement does not occur.

There must be darkness for light to exist. And where there is light, there must be darkness. For life, there must be death. Both are one and exist in polarity.

This explains why there is so much suffering in this world but also so much goodness. For why there is always a glimmer of goodness in any situation. For why we are hurt, but we seek to heal. To forgive.

For it is in understanding, forgiveness, and final acceptance that Oneness appears.

That is to say, nothing is "good" or "bad" per se but just "more or less better or worse" than something else in a given context.

But it is all perfect.

The Masculine is to search, explore, and make way.

The Feminine is to say, Home is here; you never left.

One is the mind.

One is the heart.

Both are needed for One.

A child needs its Mother.

And yet it must learn this by wa/ondering away.

One must leave to come back.

THE ART OF DOING NOTHING

Man confused and lost in thought, whether physically moving or not, is lost in life. He must "do", "become", "be something", "do something," and "go somewhere."

Man must go to war, right? He must go to work. He must look a certain way. Act a certain way? Be a certain thing?

Does he?

What must a man do when he realises he is no longer "man"?

What else *can* a man do?

Other than to be here?

In the

Am

NATURAL LAWS AND RESPONSIBILITY

Yes, but man has to pay the bills, man has to eat, and man has to raise a family, surely?

Yes, when the time comes, and if it is written, then this new man will do it.

Yet the drive isn't an illusory pull externally but a movement internal.

Just like how the flower blossoms, the bird flies, and the water ripples, he will do them.

And how dare we think we have any choice over what we do or not anyway? Leave that thinking to those who define themselves as "man".

The Eternal is an Infinite dance.

Residing in the Heart.

When in doubt.

Listen to it.

These are the natural laws.

This is responsibility.

THE EGO IS THE DEVIL

The "Ego" is all thought, for all thought has an object and a subject. One must think about something, and thus the thing doing the thinking is manifested as the "self" or "ego" as a result. The self is born. It is regarded as an obvious fact and never really examined.

Who are you? Who does the thinking? Look at the creature of thought. From where does it originate?

Thinking, and thus the nature of the ego, manifests as one's social status, gender, skin colour, flesh, and blood that we call ours. The thing that you call "you" is therefore an illusion.

Who are you when you are dreaming? Or in deep sleep? What is the canvas that allows the painting of life to exist? What is left when the I-thought vanishes?

There is only Ultimate Reality, One Truth, but thought binds man to duality, unable to see.

Ego is the Devil. It removes you from the present reality. The Eternal Infinite Timeless now. All there ever is.

But though it creates confusion in man and is a result and creator of fear, the Devil, the Ego, thought, is only "negative" when inspected under duality, when it itself manifests via thinking. When this is transcended, then it is revealed that it is also a part of One.

A misunderstood angel.

I see darkness in so many

The Devil has taken over

The light still exists

He can take no control

See him dance and he shall disappear

Only Light exists

What Ego?

I AM THE CREATOR AND THE DESTROYER. I AM.

I am the winter and the summer. I am hot and cold. I am rain and I am sun. I am up and down. I am in and out. I am life and I am death. I am stop and I am go. I am these words, I am you reading it. I am it. What you think you "are," is it. I am Allah. I am God. I am Brahman. I am Lord Shiva. I am "I". I am I am. I. am. Ohm. Aum. ॐ, ओम्, ௐ

“"Ohm" is a unit of an electric circuit that is defined as the electrical resistance between two points of a conductor when a constant potential difference of one volt, applied to these points, produces in the conductor a current of one ampere, the conductor not being the seat of any electromotive force.”

ௐ 1

. . .

ௐ 0

Alas, man has wo/wandered off adrift

Well, it is what he is led to believe.

INFINTE LOOP

Even to sustain me there must be universal consciousness
And it leads me to believe I may disappear totally.
A Big Crunch.
And yet must I not appear from somewhere?
And aren't I all things?
Don't I know that no religion, science or concept can ever contain me?
I have never left.
And yet I am always beginning.
Even to sustain me there must be universal consciousness

THE HEART RESIDES IN THE ETERNAL STATE

The Heart I speak of is not an organ, symbol, or location that exists in the material realm. It is simply the direct link mankind has to the non-dual Eternal State.

See, in duality, there is polarity, "good", "bad", subject, object. In duality, there is thinking, and thus, by extension, there is the illusory Ego and internal disturbance manifested as fear.

When the creature of thought is examined fully, the ego vanishes, as does all related fear. What is left behind? What pulls and pushes mankind if thinking does not?

The Heart. A voice that is not yours.

Like a mirror, it reflects all, attaching to nothing. With no fear, it resides in a state of bliss. All in all, whether it is recognised or not, it communicates, but the mind usually shouts over it. When the mind is understood for what it is, it will know its place and reside behind the Heart. The once whispers will begin to sing songs using a different immaterial energy. Love.

Though man has no Ultimate freewill, the choice of listening to the Heart, the most sacred, is not determined by will. When all thought disappears, there is only movement, connecting us to the purest path of all.

Whenever you're stuck on this path, simply listen to your Heart. It resides in the Eternal State.

The gut is there to protect you.

The heart to lead.

The mind to get you there.

HOW TO LISTEN TO THE HEART?

The heart sings like birds and buzzes like bees. If one is having difficulty hearing it, it's not that it stops singing; it's that our incessant thinking has drowned it out in recent times.

When the mind stops chattering, it does not suddenly trigger the heart to sing. Remember, the heart has always been singing. It is only when the mind quietens is the heart appreciated.

Thus, listening is not an active process. The understanding of thought alone is. This, if one is destined to, is done by careful, open, non-judgmental questioning of the "I" that thought originates from.

Some may find it easier than others to investigate this. But most will never think of taking this seriously. This is their destiny.

For those who try, there may be blockages in their koshas; fixing this may help.

It is essential that one lives as congruently as one can with no internal contradiction and confusion. One must live from moment to moment with no conclusions. One must live morally. Ethically. With love.

The ancients knew this. Contrary to popular belief, yoga isn't the mere process of performing a variety of stretches on a mat; no, though part of it, the word "yoga" is derived from the Sanskrit root "Yuj", meaning "to join" or "to yoke" or "to unite." It is a group of physical, mental, and spiritual practices that originated in ancient India and aim to quieten our thoughts, freeing them from mundane suffering and thus bringing about perfect harmony between the mind and body, man and nature.

Perform yoga.

Be aware that the most direct way is to question the "I." Who are you?

And if you are truly devoted and it is your destiny, then you may see.

Listen to the heart. There is no other choice. Who is listening to it?

It will be all that remains.

WHO DIES?

All fear is rooted in the fear of death. The Ultimate unknown. Thus, the fear itself is the fear of the unknown, a change of state. To fear the unknown, death - an inevitable unknown—is, by definition, irrational. Try to see this. This is highlighted even more so when one examines what death is.

Death, in the material, is purely a state of transformation on an Infinite material and non-material timeline. Everything changes. The Ego mind, however, falsely sees itself as the body, and thus death, as a threat to it. This creates fear.

One must understand that death exists only in duality. In duality, for life to exist, there must be death, yes. However, when duality is transcended, one arrives at the conclusion that there is only Eternity. Death ceases to exist.

All is One.

ALL QUESTIONS LEAD TO ONE

To ask for proof of the Ever-Present, Ever-Lasting, All-Knowing, Eternal One, is to show one's ignorance of it All.

To ask for proof of such obviousness, which is always present, is like a fish asking for proof of water. It is dependent on whether it sees it or not; that is all.

To ask is a manifestation of thought, and thus the Ego. "Someone" must be asking the question, but remember that the Ego is the very thing that must be questioned to come to True Understanding.

Using thought, man thinks the Infinite must look, act, and behave like what he knows, dualistically. But the Infinite transcends all of that. It is indescribable using words.

See how one can become very easily trapped in thought?

All questions lead to One answer. Whether directly related or not, in any language, in any form, all lead to the One. All Holy scriptures speak of the One thing.

All things are manifestations of it. Life itself is its proof.

To question, whether through words or spiritual practices, however well-intentioned, is to exist in duality and thus in ignorance.

If you are devoted to finding the Truth, before you ask anything or do anything, ask yourself, "Who" is doing the doing?

If it is written in Cosmic Law, you may one day find yourself never asking another question of this sort again.

AT THE END, THE GURU MUST TEACH HIMSELF ONLY ONCE

Once he has learnt, who has he become?
What does he see?

NO THING IS GOING TO SAVE US

As there is no "us", there is nothing to be saved.

All is perfect.

All is should be.

EVERYTHING IS PERFECT

Printed in Great Britain
by Amazon

25470950R00030